LEVERAGING ONLINE JOB PORTAL DATA IN ASIA AND THE PACIFIC

A SCOPING STUDY

MAY 2024

ASIAN DEVELOPMENT BANK

ADB

Contents

Tables and Figures

Foreword

Online job portals have transformed the way individuals seek employment; additionally, they present a wealth of data on jobs and labor market outcomes suitable for economic analysis. This report delves into the potential and challenges of utilizing near real-time data from these digital platforms. As developing economies navigate the complexities of labor market trends and shifts, as well as the demand and supply of different workforce skills, the availability of dynamic and timely information for economic analysis becomes relevant. Online job portal data can complement more traditional and time-intensive labor market surveys to develop new approaches to understand these dynamics.

However, for these data to serve as a reliable source of labor market information, there are several challenges that need to be addressed. Foremost among these concerns is that online job portal data may not be fully representative of the entire labor market, nor are they an unbiased sample. Other key issues are the quality of job portal data and the legal frameworks surrounding access to these data (e.g., data protection and privacy policies). In light of these challenges, this report examines the practical aspects of harnessing online job portal data for economic and labor market analyses.

Based on a scoping study encompassing 34 online job portal websites from 12 economies, and supplemented by interviews with industry experts, the report examines the type, structure, and format of data available for the analysis of job vacancy postings and jobseeker characteristics. This report also discusses the other considerations essential for the meaningful use and implementation of online job portal data, such as standardizing portal categorization of jobs and sectors.

We invite policymakers, economists, researchers, and stakeholders in the region to explore this report to better understand how to tap a promising data source for monitoring and analyzing evolving labor markets to help make evidence-based decisions, while shaping the future of work in Asia and the Pacific.

Albert Park
Chief Economist and Director General
Economic Research and Development Impact Department
Asian Development Bank

Acknowledgments

This report was prepared by Merl Chandana, Ayesha Zainudeen, and Imaad Muwahid of LIRNEasia; and Madhavi Pundit of the Macroeconomics Research Division under the Economic Research and Development Impact Department.

The research team involved in this project at LIRNEasia constitutes Kasun Amerasinghe, Merl Chandana, Viren Dias, Helani Galpaya, David Gunawardana, Vihanga Jayawickrama, Imaad Muwahid, and Ayesha Zainudeen. The authors are grateful for the valuable feedback received from the Asian Development Bank (ADB) team, including Daniel Boller, Ryotaro Hayashi, Minhaj U. Mahmud, Elaine S. Tan, and Priscille C. Villanueva. The authors also wish to acknowledge the contributions of the following who provided valuable insights for the research: Muhamed Bilal (National University of Computer and Emerging Sciences, Pakistan), Erin Kelley (World Bank), Shahbaz Khan (Rozee.pk), Abhishek Bhkata Shrestha (Merojob.com), Devesh Taneja (Vyre/Swaayam), and Tharindu Wijesuriya (TopJobs.lk); as well as the following staff members of the Ministry of Labor and Human Resources of Bhutan: Deki Dem, Kuenzang Lhadon, Pema Namgay, Deki Wangmo, Yangchen Wangmo, Tshering Yangki, Tashi Yangzom, and Dechen Zangmo. The grant fund for the study came from the Japan Fund for Prosperous and Resilient Asia and the Pacific, financed by the Government of Japan through ADB.

Executive Summary

There is a wealth of near real-time labor market data, which is becoming available through online job portals across Asia and the Pacific. The data has significant potential for use in economic analysis to gain an understanding of skills demand and supply, to monitor and analyze the labor market, and to study sociological and economic questions related to the labor market. However, there are challenges that need to be addressed. For example, a key concern is that the data is unlikely to provide a full and unbiased picture of the labor market—either as a whole or of any of its particular segment. This report provides insight into the practical aspects of using online job portal data for economic and labor market analysis. It examines the types of data that are available in some of the major online job portals from 12 economies in Asia and the Pacific, and discusses the potential for near real-time labor market research and analysis.

The report is based on a scoping study of major online job portals in Asia and the Pacific. It draws from a structured analysis of publicly available content on 34 online job portal websites from 12 economies and 7 key informant interviews with job portal executives and experts.

Keywords

Online job vacancy, online job portal, labor market insight, Asia Pacific

Introduction

The traditional tools of understanding job markets include labor force and skills surveys, qualitative studies, and the manual analyses of job vacancies. While these are well known for their coverage, rigor, and comparability, they often fall short in capturing the complexity, the variability, and the pace of change of labor markets at a level of granularity that is useful for policymakers and other seekers of such information. Surveys also require large amounts of resources in terms of cost and time.

In this context, online job portals (OJPs) have emerged as a promising data source that can bridge the gap. Large quantities of information are available in near real-time and often in a significant amount of detail.

OJPs vary in the range of services they provide, but broadly they include a website, which, at a minimum, lists details of employment or job vacancies for potential jobseekers. In the best case, OJPs also provide uniformly structured and detailed field-based jobseeker profiles and job vacancies, as well as advanced services such as tracking of salary trends and patterns, algorithm-driven job recommendations, and even recruiting services. The types of jobs offered usually include salaried and contract work (in the formal as well as informal sectors), and sometimes task-based gig work.[1]

OJPs offer many advantages, such as providing near real-time information on the current skills demanded by employers. They also enable comparisons across time and a wide range of occupations, industries, and geographies, as well as allow for the early detection of emerging labor market trends, thus providing jobseekers, employers, and policymakers with a forward-looking analytical tool. Further, job portals with advanced functionality often contain data about the jobseekers and their behavior on the platforms, which can provide additional insights into the supply of skills, preferences of jobseekers, and job-searching patterns on these job portals. Practical applications include the use of labor data from OJPs to identify emerging and/or high-demand occupations, skills in demand in the market, and so on. These kinds of insights have been used to inform skills policy and program design in Europe (Cedefop n.d.), Singapore (Job-Skills Insights 2022), and Indonesia (World Bank 2020). Big data for the labor market has been used in New Zealand to support indigenous workforce development and better employment outcomes for Māori (Tokona te Raki 2020); and OJP analysis has contributed to the new Pay Transparency Law in Colorado (Muhleisen et al. 2021).

However, several challenges need to be overcome before OJPs can be used to draw reliable conclusions on labor markets. A principal concern with using OJP data for economic analysis is that the data is not representative of the full job market. Not all vacancies are advertised and, even among the advertised, there are differences in coverage from one OJP to another based on their target market segment, language, approach used to collect advertisements, etc. A second major challenge is data quality. Given that the data generated on OJPs is not collected with research objectives in mind, there are no common standards for vacancy formats, schemas, and job classifications. Even within the same country, there can be sizable differences in the nature, amount, and

---

1 Gig-work platforms and websites are excluded from the scope of this study.

quality of data captured by different job portals. A third challenge is that the legal and ethical frameworks for utilizing job portal data are not always clearly established. This concern is even more pressing when personally identifiable information and other data about individuals and their behavior on job portals are available and/or used for analysis.

In the developing economies, these challenges are amplified by several factors. First, low levels of digitization can lead to systematic differences in the kinds of jobseekers who are online versus those who are not, as well as the types of employers that advertise vacancies online versus those who do not. Second, and related to low levels of digitization, low levels of digital skills can affect the levels of completeness of jobseeker profiles leading to biases in the data that is available. Furthermore, low digital skills can be associated with low levels of awareness of the potential risks of sharing large amounts of personal information online, as well as lower capacity to assess which websites are "safe" in terms of data protection. Third, higher levels of informality in the labor market can similarly lead to poor coverage of the job market (jobseekers, vacancies, and employers) by OJPs and systematic biases in the segments of the labor market that are covered on the portals.

Due to the differences in country markets and contexts, as well as the technical features of job portals, there are no standardized ways yet of conducting job portal analysis. Researchers studying OJPs employ a variety of techniques, drawing from different disciplines including statistics, econometrics, and computer science.

In this regard, it is essential that any study of job portals begins with a proper understanding of what data exists, what are the possibilities for utilizing this data to answer pertinent questions, and what are the limitations and challenges in doing so. Based on this, and guided by the objectives of the study and the availability of data, the appropriate suite of methods can be deployed to obtain reliable outputs. In this context, a scoping study was conducted to understand the type, format, and structure of data available from several job portals in Asia and the Pacific. This report, which is based on the findings of the scoping study, provides insights into the practical aspects of using OJP data for economic and labor market analysis. It lays out the practical challenges of doing so and provides recommendations for overcoming some of them. The report also identifies key areas for further research in this field, through a review of existing uses of OJP data (section 2), and a structured analysis of publicly available job vacancies in 34 OJP websites from 12 economies in Asia and the Pacific (section 3).

Review of Online Job Portal Data Use

2

This section explores how online job portal (OJP) data (both vacancy and non-vacancy) has been used for labor market analysis and reflects on its feasibility, along with examples. It then examines the limitations of OJP data and how these can be overcome, if at all.

Existing Uses of Online Job Portal Data in Research and Practice

The information captured by OJPs can be broadly categorized into two types based on their information content and the focus of past work: online job vacancy (OJV) data and non-vacancy data.

OJV data constitutes information included in a job advertisement, which can be broadly understood as an employer looking for a set of skills for performing one or more tasks. While the format and structure of this data can vary vastly, often OJV data falls into a few common categories—e.g., occupation (job title and job description), job location, skills requirements, vacancy date, and job duration—along with other variables such as wage, contract type, working conditions, etc. (Cedefop 2019).

OJVs have been extensively used for studying various skills, including soft skills, technical skills, industry-specific skills, and transferable skills. OJV analysis can reveal which skills are in demand, whether that demand is growing or declining over time, and which skills are likely to fetch higher remuneration for the worker (Xu et al. 2017, ADB and LinkedIn 2022). OJV analysis can also contribute to mapping skills to occupations (Giabelli et al. 2020) as well as identify sector- or industry-specific skills at various levels of granularity (Messum et al. 2011, Ternikov 2022). Further, OJV data can be used to improve automated job recommendations, enhance skills development curricula, and assist in talent search (Khaouja, Kassou, and Ghogho 2021; Fabo and Mýtna Kureková 2022).

Vacancy data represents a demand for skills; hence, it can be used to keep track of various dynamics in the labor market. Changes in the labor market over time, geographical distribution of jobs, demographic features, and the effect of shocks to employment can be analyzed using job vacancy data (Jony et al. 2022). Given its longitudinal nature and near real-time access, Fabo and Mýtna Kureková (2022) note that OJV data is a useful source for studying labor market changes and fluctuations in terms of number of vacancies, nature of working arrangements, wages, and impact of various shocks on the labor market (OECD 2021, Acemoglu et al. 2020, Azar et al. 2020).

OJV data has also been used by economists, sociologists, labor experts, and practitioners to test and validate hypotheses and theories related to gender discrimination and the gendered nature of skills, migration, and patterns of unemployment (Kuhn and Shen 2013; Calanca et al. 2019; Faryna et al. 2022; Mýtna Kureková and Žilinčíková 2016; Gortmaker, Jeffers, and Lee 2021).

Non-vacancy data falls broadly into three categories: (i) jobseeker data (biography, educational qualifications, skills, and past work experience), usually found in jobseeker profiles and résumé; (ii) employer data and company profile found in job advertisements on the portal; and (iii) transaction data generated by jobseekers and employers, such as numbers of clicks, numbers of applications per vacancy, timing of application, and time spent on the portal. While research studies using non-vacancy data are limited compared to vacancy data, it has the potential to unlock unique and diverse insights of labor market dynamics (Fabo and Mýtna Kureková 2022).

Non-vacancy data can be used both on its own and in combination with vacancy data to understand and reduce labor market inefficiencies by analyzing patterns of search on the portal, views, time spent, application, etc. This data can be sliced by jobseeker characteristics, sector, geography, and time of year to yield rich insights. Examples of applications include measuring labor market tightness (Adrjan and Lydon 2019) and assessing the impact of the coronavirus disease (COVID-19) pandemic on search intensity (Hensvik, Barbanchon, and Rathelot 2021). OJP data has also been increasingly used to run experimental studies for examining the impact of noncognitive (socio-emotional) skills on job market outcomes (Yamauchi et al. 2018). Analysis of transactions and portal activity can shed light on jobseekers' behavior patterns and motivations regarding applications, such as impact of jobseeker characteristics on search behavior (Matsuda et al. 2019, Lu et al. 2013).

There are several practical applications of OJP data by policymakers in relation to the labor market, even notably leading to new legislation on pay transparency (Muhleisen et al. 2021). Nitschke et al. (2021), and Fabo and Mýtna Kureková (2022) highlight several applications, which include using big data for the labor market to identify skills in demand and skill gaps in Indonesia, Malaysia, and Singapore (World Bank 2019a, 2020; Job-Skills Insights 2022); new emerging occupations in Australia (National Skills Commission, Australia 2020) and critical ones in Indonesia and Malaysia (i.e., those that are in shortage and are deemed strategic; World Bank 2019a, 2020); and "hot technologies" in the United States (Lewis and Norton 2016). The data has also been used to assess labor market exclusion toward better policies for excluded social groups, such as the Māori in New Zealand (Tokona te Raki 2020). Cedefop (or the European Centre for the Development of Vocational Training) of the European Union has developed an OJV analysis system (Cedefop n.d.) and uses big data for the labor market in vocational education training policies.

Limitations of Use and Methods to Overcome Them

While OJPs have emerged as an important source of labor market information, they come with several limitations, which need to be considered before they are used to explore labor market issues. Given the disproportionate amount of analysis conducted using vacancy data compared to non-vacancy data, the problems identified, and the solutions proposed here mainly center around vacancy data. However, they can be extended to non-vacancy data since methodological issues arising from the use of this data have common roots.

- The first major problem is *representativeness*. Online job markets provide neither a full nor accurate representation of their offline counterpart, let alone the labor market. Not all vacancies are advertised online. Some, depending on the sector and occupation type, are more likely to be advertised through traditional channels like newspapers; and some may not be advertised at all. Hiring practices differ by industry and geography and are influenced by the Internet penetration and digital skill levels of the target jobseekers. As a result, OJVs are often biased, with some sectors (e.g., software, digital marketing, etc.) and some occupation types (e.g., white-collar jobs) being overrepresented. Low-skill blue-collar jobs are often underrepresented in OJV data. This affects the extent to which findings based on the data can be generalized to the labor market. Studies have attempted to overcome the representativeness challenge by using national labor force surveys to adjust for the biases, but this method has been criticized (Mýtna Kureková et al. 2015, Fabo and Mýtna Kureková 2022). One argument is that the labor force survey data, which provides a snapshot of the job counts in the labor market, is not an accurate reflection of new job openings.

Diversifying data sources (Huang et al. 2009, Masso et al. 2016) and approaches[2] for verifying and supplementing findings from OJP analyses has been done in many studies. They limit the focus of the investigation to labor market segments that are relatively well-represented on job portals, such as software industry jobs (Bilal et al. 2017), academic jobs (Brandas, Ciprian, and Filip 2016), and entry-level student jobs (Mýtna Kureková and Žilnčíková 2016). Statistical methods have been used to reduce outliers and noise in the data to correct for biases, or to weigh the data according to a more representative data source (Turrell et al. 2019). Another approach relies on the sheer number of observations typically present in big data to act as a "self-corrective" mechanism (Mezzanzanica and Mercorio 2019).

- The second major problem has to do with the *varying quality of information sources*. OJP data are not collected with research objectives in mind. As a result, the data are not consistent or centralized, and some are even self-reported and outdated (Cedefop 2019, Fabo and Mýtna Kureková 2022). The lack of standardization in format (text, image, video, audio, etc.) and content (job titles, skill types, etc.) makes it difficult to combine, organize, and analyze data effectively without some degree of pre-processing. To compare job titles, skills, and competencies in a standardized manner, ontologies (i.e., systems of classification) need to be developed to sort and organize a diverse and complex universe of information, which is a work in progress. Other problems include (i) double counting, especially where portals aggregate vacancies from multiple sources, or employers and jobseekers use multiple portals simultaneously; and (ii) "ghost vacancies," where an online vacancy does not necessarily correspond to an actual job opening.

    While data quality issues cannot be eliminated altogether, explicitly recognizing them up front can help rectify some and, in general, inform the limitations of the inferences that can be made with a given dataset. Working toward a set of best practices in common standards is also important. This includes open-source tools and approaches (e.g., Creative Commons licenses designed to enable one to legally build upon and share the work of others), and documentation to enable comparison and reproducibility.

- The third major category of problems relates to *ethical and compliance concerns* that come with utilizing OJP data. Ethical concerns arise particularly in the context of web-scraping of OJP data. In some cases, web-scraping can be prohibited as specified in the terms and conditions of use on the websites; in others, web-scraping can negatively affect other users' experience of the portal by straining server resources of the website. While there are arguments for and against this method in the current discourse, the best practice would be to work with the consent of OJPs to obtain data for analysis.

    Privacy concerns arise because of the use of personally identifiable attributes of registered portal users. Some economies have personal data protection legislation, with provisions that govern the use of personal data on OJPs. Informed consent, obtained by way of users agreeing to the portal's terms and conditions, allows for the use of this data. However, in practice, it cannot be assumed that all jobseekers fully understand what they are giving consent to.

---

[2] For example, see stakeholder interviews in the MySkillsFuture portal.

Review of Online Job Portals in Asia and the Pacific

A structured analysis of 34 online job portals (OJPs) (including two portals with regional reach across several of the economies studied) from 12 economies in Asia and the Pacific was conducted. The economies are Bangladesh; Bhutan; Fiji; Hong Kong, China; India; Indonesia; Nepal; Pakistan; the Philippines; Singapore; Sri Lanka; and Thailand.

In each economy, the largest and most popular portals were selected, based on metrics (e.g., the number of unique visitors and site traffic) obtained from web-stats ranking sites, such as Alexa.com[3] and SimilarWeb; and cross-checked against other available sources, such as Jobboardfinder.com. Gig-work and freelancer platforms were not included, nor were social and professional networking platforms, such as LinkedIn, among others. This is because the primary purpose of platforms such as LinkedIn is not for job search, but rather for professional networking. It is through networking that users may gain the secondary benefit of being exposed to job opportunities. Furthermore, the dynamics of the gig-work market could be considerably different because of the nature of gig work (its exploration should be a separate exercise).

The objective of this scoping exercise was to understand what information can be gleaned from each of the portals to generate labor market insights through big data analytical techniques.[4]

An analysis of the structure and format of job vacancy advertisements, published on 34 portals,[5] was conducted to understand what types of online job vacancy (OJV) data are potentially available and how well-suited are they for data analytics to track labor demand. A small number of job vacancy advertisements from each of the portals being studied were examined for (i) organization and structure of content (e.g., skills requirements, job category, etc.); and (ii) format of advertisements (e.g., image versus text). Analysis of the content of these fields, such as examining how well terminology for skills or job functions listed in a vacancy post are standardized across job advertisements, was beyond the scope of this study. Thus, the analysis is not meant to be comprehensive and is not based on a large or representative set of vacancies. Approximately 5–10 vacancy posts were viewed from each portal, based on a mix of prominent positioning on the home page plus searches using terms such as software developer, finance, driver, cleaner, government jobs, etc. to obtain information about the type of data available.

For a subset of portals, an analysis of the types of information captured in a jobseeker's profile was conducted to elicit what data can potentially be used to understand the supply of skills and labor in the market, and the characteristics of jobseekers. Ten portals were selected, which met the following criteria: (i) portals, where it is possible for jobseekers to register and create profiles;[6] and (ii) portals, which either did not explicitly prohibit

---

3   As of 1 May 2022, before which the initial screening of portals was already conducted, Alexa Internet has been discontinued by its parent company, Amazon; hence, the data are no longer publicly available.

4   In practice, this kind of analysis is conditional upon all relevant and necessary permissions being obtained and safeguards being put in place.

5   These portals were from among the 36 portals initially selected in the 12 economies; two were excluded from the vacancy advertisement analysis because advertisements cannot be viewed without registering on those portals.

6   At the time of the research, several platforms did not have the facility for or require jobseekers to register and set up a profile.

registering a profile with fake information (in order to conduct research) or responded without objection to the research when contacted by the researchers.[7] Most often, an email address and/or verifiable mobile number were the primary requirements to register to use the portals as a jobseeker.

In terms of other ethical considerations, it should be noted that the content of advertisements was not extracted or used for the analysis. Similarly, no data from the jobseekers' profiles were viewed or used in the analysis. Furthermore, no job applications were lodged. In this report, portal companies are not identified by name to avoid inadvertently revealing any potentially competitive information from the portals.

To supplement the analysis, key informant interviews were conducted with seven respondents: operators of OJPs from Bhutan, India, Nepal, Pakistan, and Sri Lanka; and two researchers who had done work on OJPs or with OJP data in India and Pakistan.

The research was conducted between February and August 2022 and, therefore, reflects the structure and content of the studied portals at that time.

---

[7] To capture the data fields required to create a jobseeker profile, the researchers were required to register to use the portals. For ethical reasons, having a researcher register with their own (factual) information was not considered, so as not to affect the future use of the platforms or job search activities. Therefore, it was necessary to create a profile using fake information on these portals, which could violate the terms and conditions of use of some portals. Therefore, attempts to contact portals whose terms and conditions explicitly prohibit entering fake information were made through email, explaining the scope of the analysis. Only three responded with no objections. Those that did not respond were not included in the analysis.

Findings

Online Vacancy Data

The online vacancy advertisement analysis was conducted on 34 portals in 12 economies (Table 1 and Appendixes 1 and 3). This included two or three portals in each economy, on average, and two prominent regional portals whose reach spans between two and five of the economies studied.

Table 1: Summary of Vacancy Advertisement Formats

Portal Format	Number of Portals
Portals that allow for text format advertisements (posts)	34
Portals that also contain image format advertisements (posts)	7
Portals where image format advertisements are accompanied by standardized summary details	5

Source: Authors' observations of portal websites.

While almost all the studied portals allow for blue-collar job postings,[8] cursory searches indicate that there is a larger presence of advertisements for white-collar jobs, as the literature suggests. Key informant interviews also confirmed this. Government vacancies come up in searches in only seven of the 34 studied portals.

Some portals also include overseas job vacancy postings, especially in economies where overseas migration for work is popular, such as in Bhutan, Fiji, and the Philippines.

Format and Structure of Vacancy Advertisements

Of the 34 studied portals, 27 post job advertisements *only* in uniformly structured *text* format (Figure 1), while the remaining seven portals also include in their vacancy posts an *image* format display (Figure 2). The key distinction is how the job vacancy data is inputted and stored in the portal server. In text-format vacancies, data is entered and stored in text format in uniform, predetermined fields (e.g., for job title, job location, job description, etc.)—this data is readily machine-readable for search, sorting, and analysis. Image-format vacancies are most likely inputted as image or PDF (with vacancy information in unstandardized structure and format, using words and graphics) and stored as such; unless they are annotated in sufficient detail in the portal database, they would require one or more steps of pre-processing (including conversion to text and cleaning, at a minimum) before they can be searched, sorted, and analyzed.

---

8   Blue-collar jobs primarily involve manual labor (e.g., driver, electrician, etc.), as opposed to white-collar jobs.

Figure 1: Example of Text Format Online Job Vacancies

ABC JOBS ONLINE

Job title:	Junior software engineer	Job title:	Teaching assistant
Company	ABC Design Co	Company	Little Angels Preschool
Date posted	23 April 2023	Date posted	22 April 2023
Location	Colombo 6, Pamankade	Location	Colombo 3, Kollupitya
Salary	negotiable	Salary	
Job description	The candidate is expected to independently design websites for global clients. The candidate is expected to show up to work on time, well dressed and ready to learn. Also needs to: * Take meeting notes * Help with admin tasks * Prepare invoices for clients	Job description	Little Angels is Colombo's oldest and largest preschool. We offer a flexible working environment, we value creativity. Teaching assistants must have 3 years teaching experience and valid teaching qualifications required. Must be willing to work on weekends.
Required skills	Coding, writing, time management	Required skills	AMI or equivalent teaching diploma

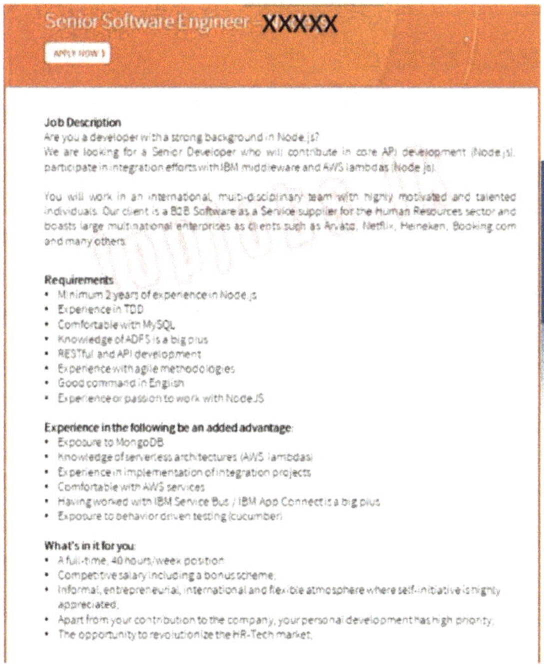

Source: Authors (for illustration purposes only).

Figure 2: Example of Image Format Online Job Vacancies

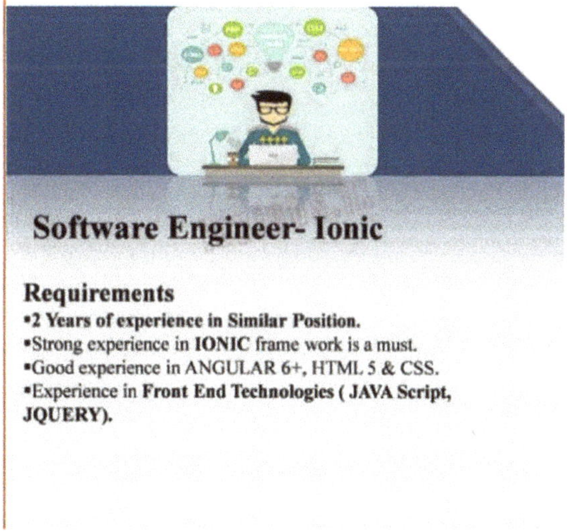

Source: TopJobs.lk.

Text Format

Text-format postings on portals, in almost all cases, consist of a set of *structured fields* and a *customized section* of the vacancy advertisement—usually the "job description." The main elements (such as the job title, location, sector, etc.) tend to be presented in structured fields, whereas, the job description section varies considerably across portals in terms of content, length, and structure (Figure 1). In some cases, the content within the job description section are arranged under distinct headings (e.g., responsibilities, required education, salary, etc.), while in others, this section is less structured. Nonetheless, in most cases, the structure is determined by the employer; hence, each posting can look different (except in one portal, where it was clear that the customizable section also had some level of standardization). As such, computational comparisons of the data in the job description fields would not be straightforward, compared to the data in the structured text fields.

Types of data fields contained in vacancy advertisements

The structured fields that were observed across portals fall into the following categories:

(1) *Job details and functions*—such as job location, number of vacancies, job title, industry, job category or functions (e.g., administration, accounting, warehousing, government job, etc.), job level (entry level, senior level, etc.), and company name. Data collected under these fields can provide insights on the location, quantity, and quality of vacancies posted on the portal.

(2) *Terms of employment*—such as whether the job is full-time or part-time, contract work, work-from-home, etc.; salary; and benefits. Data under these fields can provide insights on the quality of vacancies and salary trends.

(3) *Job requirements*—in terms of education, experience, skills, gender preferences, and other preferences (e.g., age, nationality, etc.). Skills data is especially important for skills analysis, as described in section 2.

(4) *Other fields*—such as application deadlines, number of views, and possibility of direct application, which can provide insights on the degree of jobseeker's interest, and whether labor demand and supply have been matched.

The observations are summarized in Table 2, while details can be found in Appendix 1.

Delving further into the data fields for the first category, job details and functions, all observed text-format job postings on all portals contain a job title field,[9] and most contain key fields such as company (employer) name, job location, and job level. Fields for details such as the industry and job category/functions are observed in less than half of the portals, while the number of vacancies only appears in six portals.

Under the second category, terms of employment, a field for the type of employment is provided in most portals. In some cases, this only refers to whether the job is part-time or full-time; whereas, in other cases, it refers to whether the job is contractual or permanent, and sometimes whether it is a position for remote work. The salary field is provided in almost all the portals. However, in one-third of the portals where the salary field is included in a job post, salary data are not given, or is marked as "negotiable." The inclusion of a field to present information on job benefits appears to be common in the regional portals, as well as the Bangladesh portals. Although, in many cases, it was observed that the fields did not contain any information.

---

9 The post title provides the job title either explicitly or in a more descriptive manner (e.g., "Sales representative wanted").

Table 2: Structure of Vacancy Information Observed in Online Job Portals

Vacancy Information Category	Vacancy Information Field	Number of Portals (where structured field is provided for vacancy information)
Job details and functions	Job location	30
	Number of vacancies	6
	Job title	33
	Industry	13
	Job category/functions	17
	Job level	11
	Company name	32
Terms of employment	Employment type (full-time, part-time, etc.)	30
	Salary[a]	16
	Benefits[b]	9
Requirements	Required education (level, sometimes field)	22
	Required experience (number of years)	23
	Required skills	7
	Gender preference	4
	Other stated preferences	
Others	Deadline	15
	Number of views	5
	Direct application	22

[a] In addition to these 16 portals where salary field is given in all vacancies, a further 11 portals provide salary information fields in *some* vacancy postings on the portal, but *not all*.

[b] Similarly, a further six portals provide benefits information fields in *some* vacancies, but *not all*.

Source: Authors' observation of portal websites.

For the third category, job requirements, educational requirement is specified as the level or number of completed years in some portals, and as required qualification in others, with uniformity within portals. Required experience, which is given as the number of years, is present in approximately two-thirds of the studied portals. Often, a portal would provide for both educational qualification and required experience simultaneously, rather than one or the other. On the other hand, required skills are provided less often in separate fields and in only seven portals from six different economies, usually found in the free-form job description. Specific fields for preferred gender, age, and nationality were found in a few portals (mostly in South Asia).

Out of the 34 portals, 22 enable registered jobseekers to directly apply for positions. In these instances, each time a jobseeker applies for a particular job, a data point is created. This data, when combined with jobseeker profiles and vacancy specifics, offers valuable insights into applicant job search behaviors, application patterns, and the demand for specific job categories.

Country wise, portals often display a similar level of detail in the data fields contained in a post. Portals observed in Bangladesh, India, Nepal, and Singapore tend to provide a larger number of data fields (between 10 and 13 data fields, excluding the regional portals) in a job post. In contrast, portals in Fiji and Sri Lanka provide less than half the fields in job posts but give more of the vacancy information either in the job description or within images.

The two regional portals studied tend to maintain a similar (if not identical) format and structure across economies. While both provide summary data fields (along with the customizable section), they differ in the details provided within the structured fields. One regional portal provides many of the key fields under job details and functions, terms of employment, required education, and experience (but not skills). The other provides a few fields under job details and functions and details of employment; the rest of the information is left to the customizable job description fields.

Image Format

Seven portals also allow for image-format vacancy advertisements to be posted along with text-format vacancies. For one portal in Sri Lanka, despite the text option, employers almost always opt to post image-format advertisements. In general, the image files usually originate from newspaper advertisements and government job circulars (scanned copies), particularly in Bangladesh. Further, vacancy advertisements vary considerably in structure, the amount of information provided, and the language in which they are written. All these aggregator portals, which display image vacancies, have some amount of summary data presented in a structured format; however, the details vary. For example, in the Bangladesh portals, summary data appears quite detailed for 12–13 of the 18 fields provided, compared to a bare minimum in the Sri Lanka portal. In some cases, the summary data field does not contain any useful information—for example, these may contain texts such as "refer to original advertisement below," or no text at all.

Standardization of Data Fields in Vacancy Advertisements

Analysis of the 34 studied portals, which all contain text-format vacancy advertisements, shows that six portals largely have standardized summary data, along with customized job descriptions on the vacancy, such as longer job role descriptions, skill requirements, and company descriptions (Figure 3). Fourteen portals have several

Figure 3: Level of Standardization of Vacancy Advertisements in the 34 Studied Portals

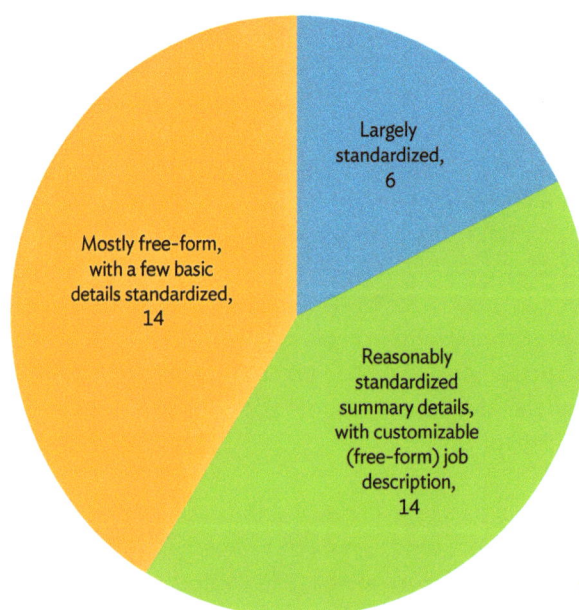

- Largely standardized, 6
- Reasonably standardized summary details, with customizable (free-form) job description, 14
- Mostly free-form, with a few basic details standardized, 14

Source: Authors' observation of portal websites.

key information fields (e.g., job title, job location, job category/functions, job type, required education, and experience) contained in a standardized format, alongside the customized job description. Of these 14 portals, many were from Bangladesh, Nepal, and Pakistan. For both groups, computational comparisons of vacancy data would be relatively simpler, than for the remaining 14 portals that displayed much of the key vacancy information within free-form job descriptions, with fewer details provided in standardized fields. Many of these portals with free-form information fields were from Bhutan, Fiji, India, Indonesia, the Philippines, and Sri Lanka.

Some of the portals, which posted image-format job vacancy advertisements, contain a relatively larger amount of summary data in standardized text fields accompanying the image files. Others, however, only have few summary text fields to accompany the image files, and therefore require more complex computational methods to analyze them.

Jobseeker Data

To understand the potential data that can be used for labor market analysis, available information from the jobseeker's profile of 10 selected portals was examined and summarized. As discussed earlier, these 10 portals were selected from the 34 studied portals based on the two criteria listed in section 3. No regional portals were selected for this jobseeker data analysis since they did not meet the second criterion. Summary observations from this analysis are presented in Table 3, while a more detailed table is presented in Appendix 2.

Format of Jobseeker Data

Across portals, key jobseeker information was required to be entered in text format through a mix of pre-coded responses (through drop-down menus), as well as text responses to be inputted into the relevant field. Information types are detailed in the next subsection.

Other data formats that portals allow jobseekers to upload include PDF documents (full resumes and work samples), images (profile pictures, scanned documents), links to other sites (social media profiles, personal websites, work samples), and videos (video profiles) (Table 3). However, these categories of data are supplementary to the key jobseeker information captured in the text fields. While the types and range of data that arise from these options increase, so does the complexity of computational analysis to extract relevant information from them.

Fields Contained in Jobseeker Profiles

The following fields were observed, some of which provide suitable data for research and analysis:

(1) *Personal information.* All the selected 10 studied portals collect jobseekers' name, date of birth, and gender, with about half the portals including a third option for gender: "other" or "transgender." Just over half provide fields for nationality and marital status. Almost all include a field where jobseekers can enter a short description of themselves and their career objectives. Some portals also include fields for religion, caste, and any disability. Data from these fields (such as non-binary gender identification, disability status, and caste) opens possibilities of examining questions of inclusion and discrimination in the labor market. Given sufficient data, this information can be used to explore which occupations or sectors are vulnerable groups more likely to be present in or absent from, what skills do these groups have, etc. One portal included fields for biometric data (e.g., blood group, height, and weight). An interesting feature of an Indian portal that was examined is the option for jobseekers to indicate career break periods. Again, this data will help to investigate and quantify the impact of career breaks for men and women on their labor market outcomes—such questions can contribute to policy decisions

Table 3: Summary of Jobseeker Data Fields Observed in Online Job Portals

Data Category	Data Field	Number of Portals Providing Specified Data Field
Personal information	Name	10
	Date of birth	10
	Gender	9
	Objective/jobseeker summary (free-form)	8
	Nationality	6
	Marital status	6
	Gender "other" option provided	5
	Family information	3
	Title (Mr., Mrs., etc.)	1
	Religion	1
	Caste	1
	Disability	1
	Biometrics (blood group, height, weight)	1
	Career break	1
Contact	Mobile	10
	Email	10
Location	Address	8
	Location (area, region, or country)	6
	Hometown/permanent address	3
	Willingness to travel or relocate	2
Identification	National ID number	3
	Passport number	2
	Passport issue date	1
	Disability ID	1
	Student number (past)	1
Education	Qualification (e.g., degree)	10
	Institution	9
	Dates	7
	Specialization/field of study	6
	Grades, GPA, etc.	4
	Description (free-form)	2
	School education (qualifications, results, etc.)	2
	Location	2
	Course language	1
Current job	Job title	4
	Organization (current or last)	3
	Salary	3
	Description	3
	Notice period	3
	Job category	2
	Dates	2
	Employment status (working, unemployed, student)	1
	Job level	1
	Freelancer salary/rates	1
	Industry	1

continued on next page

Table 3 *continued*

Data Category	Data Field	Number of Portals Providing Specified Data Field
Work history	Job title	9
	Organization	9
	Dates	9
	Description (free-form)	7
	Industry	5
	Job level	3
	Job category	3
	Job location	3
	Awards/achievements	3
	Project/portfolio details	3
	Reference	3
	Professional certifications/memberships	3
	Number of years	2
	Research area/description	2
	Responsibilities	2
	Job type (full-time, part-time, internship)	1
Expected	Salary	7
	Location	5
	Job title	4
	Job type (full-time, part-time, internship)	4
	Job level	3
	Job category	3
	Organization type/sector/industry	3
	Specific availability (hours per days of the week)	1
Skills	Title/type	8
	Languages	5
	Languages proficiency	5
	Level/proficiency	4
	Experience (years)	1
	Driving license	1
	Training details (title, organization, dates, duration)	1
	Software competency	1
Ability to perform job	Vehicle possession	1
	Foreign work permit	1
	Willing to use TimeProof	1
Online profile	Social media/professional networking link	7
	Website/online profile	4
Uploads	Photo	10
	CV/resume	5
	Portfolio/work samples (or links to them)	2
	Video profile	2
	Government ID (scanned)	1

CV = curriculum vitae, ID = identification, GPA = grade point average.
Source: Authors' observation of portal websites.

on maternity and paternity benefit legislation, as well as childcare subsidization. Given the nature of much of this personal information, privacy breach risks can be overcome through anonymization and aggregation of the data during analysis.

(2)   *Contact information*. All portals require jobseekers to provide a mobile contact number and/or an email address to complete the registration. Once again, to prevent privacy breaches, this kind of information would need to be removed from the datasets prior to research.

(3)   *Location*. All portals include fields for the jobseeker's location, either in the form of a full address or the area or region in which they are located. Geographic location data can provide policy-relevant insights into where jobs are available versus where workers with skills are available, as well as geographic wage patterns.

(4)   *Identification information*. Some portals include fields for details contained in national identification documents, such as a national identity number, passport number, disability ID number, and sometimes for a scanned version of the national identity document. It may be that the information is collected for verifying that the jobseeker is real or for other reasons. Regardless, caution should be taken with this data because of privacy risks and surveillance risks, especially among vulnerable populations. Subject to appropriate safeguards (including but not limited to informed consent, anonymization, etc.), in theory, such data can be merged with other large datasets containing national identification data to expand the possibilities of analysis. An example is combining datasets from the education domain with online job datasets to implement vocational training and education curricula development and policy.

(5)   *Education information*. Almost all portals include fields for information on the jobseeker's educational qualifications and awarding institutions, usually along with the start and completion dates, as well as the specialization of study. A small number of portals ask for the jobseeker's final grade, grade point average (GPA), or equivalent score. This kind of data is useful to understand the characteristics of labor and the role that education plays in labor market outcomes. Analyzed in conjunction with other demographic data, the information can also provide insights for education policy.

(6)   *Work history* (including current job). All portals include fields for previous (and current) job titles, organization names, and associated periods of employment. Often, a field is included for a description of the job role and responsibilities. Sometimes, details such as industry, job level, job category, and location are elicited. A few portals allow for the inclusion of details such as awards and achievements, past projects,[10] and professional certifications. Work history data similarly provides insights into the supply of labor, and perhaps can also track the career trajectory of various demographics and job sectors. This could help identify segments that may require some form of targeted assistance to sustain their participation in the labor market (e.g., women and those belonging to specific castes, geographies, etc.).

(7)   *Expected work conditions*. Many of the portals include a field for the jobseekers to input their expected salary. A few include fields related to job preferences, including location, title, type (e.g., full-time or part-time), level, category, and industry. Such information can provide insights into the geographical patterns of demand for jobs, or which occupations and sectors are in demand and on what terms. Combined with jobseekers' demographic information, this can be insightful for jobs in demand among different demographic groups.

---

[10] This data field may include academic projects and/or work-related projects, although it is usually not specified.

(8) *Skills*. Most portals include fields for jobseekers to enter their skills (if not already included in the summary description). They include technical skills related to the job, software capabilities, and soft skills. Some portals additionally ask jobseekers to indicate their level of proficiency in a selected list of skills. One portal offers a skills diagnostic test, the results of which can be included in the jobseeker's profile. Several portals have fields for language capabilities and level of proficiency. Insights into the current skills composition of the labor force, together with online job vacancy (OJV) data on skills demand, can help identify skills gaps, emerging skills, etc. These insights can guide the design of vocational education policy including, but not limited to, curricula design. Combined with other data on demographics, location, sector, etc., this information can help to better allocate vocational education resources.

(9) *Other capabilities*. Other specific fields are included in some portals for jobseekers to indicate whether they own a vehicle (e.g., two- or four-wheeler), and whether they possess any foreign work permits.

(10) *Other forms of data*. All the observed portals include an option to provide a profile photo, and many include the facility to upload a detailed résumé, work portfolio, and work samples. Some portals include the option to add a video profile. Many portals provide jobseekers the option of linking their account to their social media and professional networking profiles or to provide links to their own websites. As mentioned earlier, the more detailed the data, the more complex the computational analysis becomes.

Challenges of Using Jobseeker Data for Labor Market Insights

Almost all the selected 10 studied portals capture a basic amount of personal information, as well as information on the jobseeker's location, educational qualifications, work history, and even skills data. The potential uses of the kinds of data collected have been discussed above. Although there is some standardization in the fields that are provided for jobseekers to enter their information into, quantitative comparison of the data within and between portals may not be straightforward for several reasons:

(1) Some portals capture the data in pre-coded responses, while others allow the jobseeker to enter information in free-form text, especially for fields relating to skills, educational qualifications, and job titles. Free-form text makes analysis both within and between portals more challenging. Unstructured, free-form text inherently requires more sophisticated techniques of natural language processing for reliable information retrieval. Further, many of the portals studied include fields where the jobseekers can write down (in free form) a short description of themselves or their career objectives, again making computational comparisons less straightforward.

(2) The degree of granularity based on geographic information varies considerably across portals. For instance, some portals allow jobseekers to enter their complete address, line by line, while others only ask for the location by region.

(3) Another problem relates to missing data, which has an impact on the extent to which data insights can be generalized. This is because of variation across portals in the fields that are mandatory versus optional. In some portals, one can register with a name, email address, and/or mobile number, and then proceed to use the portal. Other portals contain a larger number of mandatory fields, many of which may not be applicable for certain categories of jobseekers, and some jobseekers might choose not to complete every field. Missing data introduces systematic biases in the analysis. Certain types and categories of jobseekers are more likely than others to have missing data—for instance, women are well known to be time-poor (UN Women 2020) and less proficient in digital skills (West et al. 2019). Accordingly, a higher share of women versus men could be expected to have incomplete

profiles (missing data); consequently, women are likely to be underrepresented in many data fields in a job portal. Portals often encourage jobseekers to add more information to their profile, indicating that this would increase their visibility among employers and improve job recommendations made by portals.

(4)   A few portals include data fields, which can potentially capture rich information that can be used to explore a variety of pertinent socioeconomic issues, such as inclusion and discrimination. For example, data on non-binary gender identification and disability status can be used to delve into questions about labor market characteristics and experiences of vulnerable groups. However, these data are likely to suffer from selection biases.

(5)   Certain types of data that are collected will have implications for data protection legislation compliance. In addition to data collection, sharing and processing of data (by the data collector as well as third parties) must comply with the relevant legislation of the territory from which it comes (e.g., informed consent, pseudonymization of personally identifiable and other sensitive information, etc.).

Conclusion

There is a wealth of near real-time labor market data, which is becoming available through online job portals (OJPs) across Asia and the Pacific. Given the large amount of data available within OJPs, there is much potential for use in labor market and broader socioeconomic analyses. Analysis of OJP data can contribute to skills analyses, labor market monitoring, as well as understanding of other socioeconomic issues (e.g., wage discrimination). The data can also enable research on job search behavior and labor market tightness. While these studies can contribute to a wider, more nuanced, and timely understanding of labor market dynamics, importantly, it can also contribute toward policy development and program design.

This study sought to understand what information can be gleaned from each of the portals examined to generate labor market insights through big data analytical techniques. Analysis of the structure and format of vacancy advertisements on 34 portals showed a predominance of text-format vacancies; although, some portals also provided vacancies in image format. Images require more complex computational processes to analyze on a large scale compared to text; therefore, separate processes would need to be followed to do so. Among portals that provide text-format advertisements, there is a range of standardization of the key information fields provided in advertisements. Most portals either moderately or largely standardize, potentially making computational comparison at scale relatively easy—although, where free-form job descriptions are provided, analysis would be a little more complex.

An analysis of the types of information captured in a jobseeker's profile on 10 selected portals was conducted to elicit what types of data can potentially be used to understand the supply of skills and labor in the market, and the characteristics of jobseekers. Key jobseeker information (such as demographics, education, and skill information) can be entered in text format on all portals, through a mix of pre-coded responses and text responses in the relevant fields. Supplementary data can also be uploaded in various other formats (e.g., full résumés, profile photographs, links to social media, etc.). All 10 selected portals capture a basic amount of personal and contact information, as well as information on the jobseeker's location, educational qualifications, and work history. Skills data is captured by almost all the 10 portals examined. Several portals also capture various aspects of the jobseeker's preferences or expectations, such as their expected salary, as well as the job location, sector, title, etc.

While there are many advantages for economic analysis using this data, a major concern is that OJP data will be unable to provide a full and unbiased picture of the labor market—either in whole or any specific segment. Another issue is that systematic biases from missing data on the jobseeker and on vacancies will affect the representativeness of OJP data. Further concerns relate to the variability in the structure and format of the data available within OJPs, which make quantitative comparisons within and between portals more complex. While section 4 describes the kinds of data available on portals and some of their potential uses, the limitations and biases of the datasets should be acknowledged.

Therefore, selection of a portal as a data source should primarily be guided by the research question being studied. It is important that the right research questions are being asked from the data at hand. Further, validation is important (Fabo and Mýtna Kureková 2022). For example, with OJP data, inferences about the general labor market can be made in the event of an accompanying, well-designed survey of new vacancies done on the full population to make the right statistical adjustments. If the goal of a study is to understand labor market trends, rather than inference, there is room for analyzing OJP data even in the absence of statistical correction based on surveys. In most settings, a short, exploratory pilot study would be a good first step to understand the limitations of the data from identified sources, the relevant labor market context, and other practical challenges of doing labor market analysis within a given country.

Regional job portals could be promising partners for collaborative work, given their advanced functionality, sophisticated tools, and previous experience working with policymakers and labor market practitioners. While these portals may contain relatively fewer standardized data fields than the country-specific portals, information collected from both the vacancy and the jobseeker side is relatively consistent across domains, facilitating cross-country analysis. Regional portals also usually have well-developed application programming interface for streamlined data access, and their presence in multiple economies allow for better regional comparisons. However, as has been noted in this report, regional portals may be biased toward specific types of jobs.

Further research is needed to understand the extent to which portal categorization of jobs and sectors can be mapped with a common standard, such as the European Skills, Competences, Qualifications and Occupations (ESCO);[11] other national statistical office categorizations; and O*NET.[12] This would allow for easier merging of and comparison between datasets. Collaboration with portals (especially nascent ones) to work toward standardizing categorizations would be a useful venture.

Given the predominance of an informal sector and blue-collar jobs in many of the developing economies in this study, similar research should be undertaken to include the emerging blue-collar job portals. Further, with an increasing uptake of nonstandard forms of work like gig work and online freelancing, the analysis could be extended to gig-work platforms and professional networking websites. This could potentially provide insights into actual work hours, skills, and income potential. Considering that these forms of work are sometimes taken up in addition to standard employment, the problem of double counting of jobseekers across platforms would need to be overcome.

Finally, given the large amounts of personally identifiable information that the portals collect, OJP data would be subject to appropriate data-sharing collaborations, along with consent, data protection, and adherence to privacy obligations. Therefore, as a precursor to any data collaborations, a legal analysis would be required of (i) the terms and conditions, as well as the privacy policies of these portals; and (ii) the data protection legislation and regulations of the territory in which the portal operates. This will help ascertain whether the data collected can be shared, used, and processed directly, or would require further agreements between data providers and researchers.

---

11 European Commission. 2013. ESCO Taxonomy – Classification of European Skills, Competences, Qualifications and Occupations just released. *Cedefop*. 4 November.
12 O*NET OnLine. https://www.onetonline.org/.

Vacancy Data Fields (y = yes; s = present in some vacancies only)

Anonymized Portal ID	Text	Image	Images Accompanied by Standardized Summary Details	Newspaper Ads/Other Circulars Also Posted	Blue Collar	White Collar	Government Jobs	Job Location	Number of Vacancies	Job Title	Industry	Job Category/Functions	Job Level	Company Name	Employment Type (FT, PT, etc.)	Salary	Benefits	Required Education (Level; Sometimes Field)	Required Experience (Number of Years)	Required Skills	Gender Percentage	Other Stated Preferences	Deadline	Number of Views	Direct Application
								Job Details and Functions							Terms of Employment			Requirements					Others		
Nepal portal 1	Text	Image	y	y		y		y	y	y		y	y	y	y	y		y	y				y	y	n
Nepal portal 2	Text					y		y	y	y		y	y	y	y	y		y	y				y		y
Nepal portal 3	Text	Image	y	y	y	y	y	y		y*	y	y	y	y	y	y		y	y	y	y		y	y	y
Pakistan portal 1	Text	Image	y	y	y	y	y	y			y	y		y	y	s		y					y		y
Pakistan portal 2	Text				y	y		y	y					y	y	s		y					y		y
Pakistan portal 3	Text					y		y	y	y	y			y	y	s		y	y	y		Age	y	y	y
Bangladesh portal 1	Text	Image	n	y	y	y		y				y		y	y	y	y	y				In "other requirements" fields			y
Bangladesh portal 2	Text	Image	y	y	?	y	y	y	y	y	y	y		y	y	y	y	y	y	y	y	Age	y		
Bangladesh portal 3	Text	Image	y	y	y	y	y	y	y	y	y			y	y	y	y	y	y			Age	y		
India portal 1	Text				y	y		y		y	y	y	y	y	y			y	y		y				y
India portal 2	Text				y	y		y		y	y	y		y	y	s	s	y							y
India portal 3	Text				y	y		y		y	y	y		y	y	s	s	y	y	y	y				
Philippines portal 1	Text				y	y		y		y	y	y	y	y	y	s	y	y	y	y					y
Philippines portal 2	Text				y	y		y				y		y	y	s	s								n
Philippines portal 3	Text				y	y				y				y	y	y		y		y					y
Bhutan portal 1	Text				y	y		y	y	y	y	y		y		y		y	y				y	y	
Bhutan portal 2	Text	Image	*	*		y	y	y	y		y	y		y	y	y		y	y						y
Bhutan portal 3	Text	Image	**		y	y		y	y	y		y		y				y					y		y

continued on next page

Appendix 1 *table continued*

Anonymized Portal ID	Text	Image	Images Accompanied by Standardized Summary Details	Newspaper Ads/Other Circulars Also Posted	Blue Collar	White Collar	Government Jobs	Job Location	Number of Vacancies	Job Title	Industry	Job Category/Functions	Job Level	Company Name	Employment Type (FT, PT, etc.)	Salary	Benefits	Required Education (Level; Sometimes Field)	Required Experience (Number of Years)	Required Skills	Gender Percentage	Other Stated Preferences	Deadline	Number of Views	Direct Application
Fiji portal 1	Text				y	y		y		y	y	y		y	y										y
Fiji portal 2	Text				y	y	?			y	y			y	y	y			y			Nationality	y		
Indonesia portal 1	Text				y	y		y		y	y	y	y	y	y	s	y		y						y
Indonesia portal 2	Text				y			y		y				y	y	s	s								n
Indonesia portal 3	Text				y	y	y	y		y		y		y	y			y	y						y
Sri Lanka portal 1	(Text)	Image	y	y						y													y	y	
Sri Lanka portal 2	Text				y	y				y				y	y	s		y	y				y		s
Sri Lanka portal 3	Text							y		y				y									y		
Thailand portal 1	Text				y	y		y		y				y	y										y
Thailand portal 2	Text				y	y		y		y				y	y	y	y	y	y		y	Age			s
Thailand portal 3	Text				y			y		y	y	y	y	y	y			y	y						y
Hong Kong, China portal 1	Text				y			y		y	y	y	y	y	y			y	y						y
Hong Kong, China portal 2	Text				y	y	y	y		y				y	y	s	s								n
Hong Kong, China portal 3	Text				y	y		s		y	y	y	y	y	y	s	y	y	y	y					y
Singapore portal 1	Text				y	y		y		y	y	y	y	y	y			y	y	y					
Singapore portal 2	Text				y	y		y		y	y	y	y	y	y				y				y		y

? = could not be ascertained, FT = full-time, PT = part-time.

* Could not be ascertained.

** Initial research (January–March 2022) showed image-format posts, but an examination in November 2022 showed only structured image-format posts.

Source: Authors' observation of portal websites.

Jobseeker Data Fields in Online Job Portals

Data Category	Data Field	Nepal Portal 2	Nepal Portal 3	Pakistan Portal 1	Pakistan Portal 3	Bangladesh Portal 1	India Portal 1	Philippines Portal 3	Sri Lanka Portal 1	Sri Lanka Portal 2	Sri Lanka Portal 3	Number of Portals Providing Specified Data Field
Personal information	Name	■	■	■	■	■	■	■	■	■	■	10
	Date of birth	■	■	■	■	■	■	■	■	■	■	10
	Gender		■	■	■	■	■	■	■	■	■	9
	Objective/jobseeker summary (free-form)	■	■		■	■	■	■		■	■	8
	Nationality			■	■	■		■		■	■	6
	Marital status	■		■	■	■			■	■		6
	Gender "other" option provided	■	■		■			■		■		5
	Family information				■		■		■			3
	Title (Mr., Mrs., etc.)						■					1
	Religion						■					1
	Caste						■					1
	Disability						■					1
	Biometrics (blood group, height, weight)						■					1
	Career break							■				1
Contact	Mobile	■	■	■	■	■	■	■	■	■	■	10
	Email	■	■	■	■	■	■	■	■	■	■	10
Location	Address	■	■		■	■	■		■	■	■	8
	Location (area, region, or country)	■	■	■			■			■	■	6
	Hometown/permanent address		■	■			■					3
	Willingness to travel or relocate				■		■					2
Identification	National ID number				■	■			■			3
	Passport number					■			■			2
	Passport issue date								■			1
	Disability ID						■					1
	Student number (past)							■				1

continued on next page

Appendix 2 *table continued*

Data Category	Data Field	Nepal Portal 2	Nepal Portal 3	Pakistan Portal 1	Pakistan Portal 3	Bangladesh Portal 1	India Portal 1	Philippines Portal 3	Sri Lanka Portal 1	Sri Lanka Portal 2	Sri Lanka Portal 3	Number of Portals Providing Specified Data Field
Education	Qualification (e.g., degree)	■	■	■	■	■	■	■	■	■	■	10
	Institution	■	■	■	■	■	■		■	■	■	9
	Dates	■	■		■	■	■		■	■		7
	Specialization/field of study				■	■	■		■	■	■	6
	Grades, GPA, etc.				■				■	■	■	4
	Description (free-form)	■							■			2
	School education (qualifications, results, etc.)					■	■					2
	Location					■			■			2
	Course language								■			1
Current job	Job title		■				■	■	■			4
	Organization (current or last)		■				■		■			3
	Salary					■	■		■			3
	Description		■			■			■			3
	Notice period						■		■	■		3
	Job category		■						■			2
	Dates								■	■		2
	Employment status (working, unemployed, student)									■		1
	Job level				■							1
	Freelancer salary/rates				■							1
	Industry						■					1
Work history	Job title	■	■	■	■	■	■		■	■	■	9
	Organization	■	■	■	■	■	■		■	■	■	9
	Dates	■	■	■	■	■	■		■	■	■	9
	Description (free-form)	■	■		■	■	■		■	■		7
	Industry				■	■	■		■	■		5
	Job level				■				■	■		3
	Job category				■			■		■		3
	Job location					■	■			■		3
	Awards/achievements				■		■		■			3
	Project/portfolio details				■		■		■			3
	Reference				■				■	■		3
	Professional certifications/memberships				■		■		■			3
	Numbers of years				■		■					2
	Research (area/description)						■	■				2
	Responsibilities					■	■					2
	Job type (full-time, part-time, internship)						■					1

continued on next page

Appendix 2 *table continued*

Data Category	Data Field	Nepal Portal 2	Nepal Portal 3	Pakistan Portal 1	Pakistan Portal 3	Bangladesh Portal 1	India Portal 1	Philippines Portal 3	Sri Lanka Portal 1	Sri Lanka Portal 2	Sri Lanka Portal 3	Number of Portals Providing Specified Data Field
Expected work conditions	Salary	X	X		X	X	X	X	X			7
	Location	X	X			X	X	X				5
	Job title				X	X				X		4
	Job type (full-time, part-time, shift)	X	X			X	X					4
	Job level	X	X				X					3
	Job category	X	X				X					3
	Organization type/sector/industry		X			X	X					3
	Specific availability (hours per day, days of week)						X					1
Skills	Title/type	X	X	X	X	X	X		X	X		8
	Languages	X	X		X	X			X			5
	Languages proficiency	X	X		X	X			X			5
	Level/proficiency	X			X		X			X		4
	Experience (years)		X									1
	Driving license		X									1
	Training details (title, organization, dates, duration)		X									1
	Software competency						X					1
Ability to perform job	Vehicle possession		X									1
	Foreign work permit								X			1
	Willing to use TimeProof							X				1
Online profile	Social media/professional networking link	X	X		X			X	X	X	X	7
	Website/online profile	X	X							X	X	4
Uploads	Photo	X	X	X	X	X	X	X	X	X	X	10
	CV/resume	X	X			X				X		5
	Portfolio/work samples (or links to them)									X		2
	Video profile				X	X						2
	Government ID (scanned)						X					1

CV = curriculum vitae, GPA = grade point average, ID = identification.
Source: Authors' observation of portal websites.

APPENDIX 3
List of Online Job Portals

Jobseeker Data Analysis

1.	Bangladesh	bdjobs
2.	Sri Lanka	Ikman Jobs
3.	Sri Lanka	Jobeka.lk
4.	Nepal	Jobsnepal.com
5.	Pakistan	Jobz.pk
6.	Nepal	Kumarijob
7.	India	Naukri
8.	Philippines	Onlinejobs.ph
9.	Pakistan	Rozee.pk
10.	Sri Lanka	Topjobs.lk

Vacancy Analysis

1.	Bangladesh	Bdgovtjob.net	18.	India	Jobsforher
2.	Bangladesh	bdjobs	19.	Nepal	Jobsnepal.com
3.	Bangladesh	BDJobsCareers	20.	Philippines	JobStreet
4.	Hong Kong, China	Ctgoodjobs	21.	Indonesia	Jobstreet
5.	Indonesia	Disnakerja.com	22.	Singapore	JobStreet
6.	Bhutan	Dziseldra.com	23.	Thailand	Jobthai
7.	Sri Lanka	Ikman Jobs	24.	Pakistan	Jobz.pk
8.	Pakistan	Indeed	25.	Nepal	Kumarijob
9.	India	Indeed	26.	Nepal	Merojobs
10.	Philippines	Indeed	27.	Bhutan	MOLHR
11.	Indonesia	Indeed	28.	Singapore	Mycareersfuture
12.	Hong Kong, China	Indeed	29.	Fiji	Myjobsfiji.com
13.	Bhutan	Job-a Job-a	30.	India	Naukri
14.	Thailand	JobBKK	31.	Philippines	Onlinejobs.ph
15.	Sri Lanka	Jobeka.lk	32.	Pakistan	Rozee.pk
16.	Thailand	JobsDB	33.	Sri Lanka	Topjobs.lk
17.	Hong Kong, China	JobsDB	34.	Fiji	Vacanciesinfiji.com

References

Acemoglu, D.; D. Autor; J. Hazell; and P. Restrepo. 2020. AI and Jobs: Evidence from Online Vacancies. *NBER Working Paper Series No. 28257*. National Bureau of Economic Research, Inc. https://ideas.repec.org/p/nbr/nberwo/28257.html.

Adrjan, P. and R. Lydon. 2019. Clicks and Jobs: Measuring Labor Market Tightness Using Online Data. *Economic Letter Series, 2019* (6). Central Bank of Ireland. https://www.centralbank.ie/docs/default-source/publications/economic-letters/vol-2019-no-6-clicks-and-jobs-measuring-labour-market-tightness-using-online-data-(adrjan-and-lydon).pdf.

Asian Development Bank (ADB) and LinkedIn. 2022. *Digital Jobs and Digital Skills: A Shifting Landscape in Asia and the Pacific.* Manila. http://dx.doi.org/10.22617/SPR220348.

Azar , J.; I. Marinescu; M. Steinbaum; and B. Taska. 2020. Concentration in US Labor Markets: Evidence from Online Vacancy Data. *Labour Economics*. (66). 101886. https://doi.org/10.1016/j.labeco.2020.101886.

Bilal, M.; N. Malik; M. Khalid; and M. I. Lali. 2017. Exploring Industrial Demand Trends in Pakistan Software Industry Using Online Job Portal Data. *University of Singh Journal of Information and Communication Technology*. 1(1). pp. 17–24. https://journals.indexcopernicus.com/api/file/viewByFileId/379197.pdf.

Brandas, C.; P. Ciprian; and F.G. Filip. 2016. Data Driven Decision Support Systems: An Application Case in Labour Market Analysis. *Romanian Journal of Information Science and Technology*. 19(1–2). pp. 65–77. https://www.imt.ro/romjist/Volum19/Number19_1-2/pdf/05-FFilip.pdf.

Calanca, F.; L. Sayfullina; L. Minkus; C. Wagner; and E. Malmi. 2019. Responsible Team Players Wanted: An Analysis of Soft Skill Requirements in Job Advertisements. *EPJ Data Science*. 8(1). pp. 1–20. https://doi.org/10.1140/epjds/s13688-019-0190-z.

Cedefop. 2019. *Online Job Vacancies and Skills Analysis: A Cedefop Pan-European Approach*. Cedefop Publications Office. http://data.europa.eu/doi/10.2801/097022.

Cedefop. n.d. European Centre for the Development of Vocational Training. https://www.cedefop.europa.eu/en.

Fabo, B. and L. Mýtna Kureková. 2022. Methodological Issues Related to the Use of Online Labor Market Data. *ILO Working Paper 68*. International Labour Organization. https://www.ilo.org/global/publications/working-papers/WCMS_849357/lang--en/index.htm.

Faryna, O.; T. Pham; O. Talavera; and A. Tsapin. 2022. Wage and Unemployment: Evidence from Online Job Vacancy Data. *Journal of Comparative Economics*. 50(1). pp. 52–70. https://doi.org/10.1016/j.jce.2021.05.003.

Giabelli, A.; L. Malandri; F. Mercorio; and M. Mezzanzanica. 2020. GraphLMI: A Data Driven System for Exploring Labor Market Information through Graph Databases. *Multimedia Tools and Applications*. 81. 3061–3090. https://doi.org/10.1007/s11042-020-09115-x.

Gortmaker, J.; J. Jeffers; and M. Lee. 2021. Labor Reactions to Credit Deterioration: Evidence from LinkedIn Activity. *SSRN Scholarly Paper ID 3456285*. Social Science Research Network. https://doi.org/10.2139/ssrn.3456285.

Hensvik, L.; T. Le Barbanchon; and R. Rathelot. 2021. Job Search during the COVID-19 Crisis. *Journal of Public Economics*. 194. 104349. https://doi.org/10.1016/j.jpubeco.2020.104349.

Huang, H.; L. Kvasny; K. Joshi; E. M. Trauth; and J. Mahar. 2009. Synthesizing IT Job Skills Identified in Academic Studies, Practitioner Publications and Job Ads. *SIGMIS CPR '09: Proceedings of the Special Interest Group on Management Information System's 47th Annual Conference on Computer Personnel Research*. pp. 121–128. https://doi.org/10.1145/1542130.1542154.

Jony, S. S. R.; T. Kano; R. Hayashi; N. Matsuda; and M. S. Rahman. 2022. An Exploratory Study of Online Job Portal Data of the ICT Sector in Bangladesh: Analysis, Recommendations and Preliminary Implications for ICT Curriculum Reform. *Education Sciences*. 12(7). p. 423. http://dx.doi.org/10.3390/educsci12070423.

Khaouja, I.; I. Kassou; and M. Ghogho. 2021. A Survey on Skill Identification from Online Job Ads. *IEEE Access*. 9. 118134–118153. https://doi.org/10.1109/ACCESS.2021.3106120.

Kuhn, P. and K. Shen. 2013. Gender Discrimination in Job Ads: Evidence from China. *The Quarterly Journal of Economics*. 128(1). pp. 287–336. http://hdl.handle.net/10.1093/qje/qjs046.

Lewis, P. and J. Norton. 2016. *Identification of "Hot Technologies" within the O*NET® System*. O*NET Resource Center. https://www.onetcenter.org/reports/Hot_Technologies.html.

Lu, Y.; S. Ingram; and D. Gillet. 2013. A Recommender System for Job Seeking and Recruiting Website. *WWW '13 Companion: Proceedings of the 22nd International Conference on World Wide Web*. pp. 963–966. https://doi.org/10.1145/2487788.2488092.

Masso, J.; L. Mýtna Kureková; M. Tverdostup; and Z. Žilinčíková. 2016. *Return Migration Patterns of Young Return Migrants after the Crisis in the CEE Countries: Estonia and Slovakia*. Centre for Research on Management and Employment. https://www.voced.edu.au/content/ngv%3A77741.

Matsuda, N.; T. Ahmed; and S. Nomura. 2019. Labor Market Analysis Using Big Data: The Case of a Pakistani Online Job Portal. *World Bank Policy Research Working Paper No. 9063*. http://hdl.handle.net/10986/32672.

Messum, D.; L. Wilkes; and D. Jackson. 2011. Employability Skills: Essential Requirements in Health Manager Vacancy Advertisements. *Asia Pacific Journal of Health Management*. 6(2). pp. 22–28. https://search.informit.org/doi/pdf/10.3316/ielapa.405517595697217?download=true.

Messum, D.; L. Wilkes; K. Peters; and D. Jackson. 2016. Content Analysis of Vacancy Advertisements for Employability Skills: Challenges and Opportunities for Informing Curriculum Development. *Journal of Teaching and Learning for Graduate Employability*. 7(1). pp. 72–86. https://doi.org/10.21153/jtlge2016vol7no1art582.

Mezzanzanica, M. and F. Mercorio. 2019. *Big Data for Labour Market Intelligence: An Introductory Guide*. European Training Foundation. https://www.etf.europa.eu/en/publications-and-resources/publications/big-data-labour-market-intelligence-introductory-guide.

Muhleisen, M. B.; D.L. Zwisler; and R. Chacon. 2021. Colorado Revises Guidance on Job Posting Requirements. *Society for Human Resource Management*. https://www.shrm.org/resourcesandtools/legal-and-compliance/state-and-local-updates/pages/colorado-revises-guidance-on-job-posting-requirements.aspx.

Mýtna Kureková, L.; M. Beblavý; and A. Thum-Thysen. 2015. Using Online Vacancies and Web Surveys to Analyse the Labor Market: A Methodological Inquiry. *IZA Journal of Labor Economics*. 4(1). pp. 1–20. https://doi.org/10.1186/s40172-015-0034-4.

Mýtna Kureková, L. and Z. Žilinčíková. 2016. Are Student Jobs Flexible Jobs? Using Online Data to Study Employers' Preferences in Slovakia. *IZA Journal of European Labor Studies*. 5(1). pp. 1–14. https://doi.org/10.1186/s40174-016-0070-5.

National Skills Commission, Australia. 2020. *Emerging Occupations: How New Skills Are Changing Australian Jobs.* https://www.nationalskillscommission.gov.au/sites/default/files/2021-12/Emerging%20occuptations_How%20new%20skills%20are%20changing%20Australian%20jobs_0.pdf.

Nitschke, J.; L. O'Kane; B. Taska; and N. Hodge. 2021. Big Data for the Labor Market: Sources, Uses and Opportunities. *Issues Paper No. 13*. Asia-Pacific Economic Cooperation (APEC) Secretariat, APEC Policy Support Unit. https://www.apec.org/publications/2021/12/big-data-for-the-labor-market-sources-uses-and-opportunities.

Organisation for Economic Co-operation and Development (OECD). 2021. An Assessment of the Impact of COVID-19 on Job and Skills Demand Using Online Job Vacancy Data. *OECD Policy Responses to Coronavirus (COVID-19)*. OECD Publishing. https://doi.org/10.1787/20fff09e-en.

Skills Future Singapore. 2022. Skills Demand for the Future Economy 2023/24. https://www.skillsfuture.gov.sg/skillsreport.

Ternikov, A. 2022. Soft and Hard Skills Identification: Insights from IT Job Advertisements in the CIS Region. *PeerJ Computer Science.* 8. https://doi.org/10.7717/peerj-cs.946.

Tokona te Raki. 2020. *Regional and National Employment and Skills Report.* (Retrieved 8 June 2022). http://www.maorifutures.co.nz/wp-content/uploads/2020/08/Te-Kete-Pukenga-Wh%C4%81nau-Report.pdf.

Turrell, A.; B. Speigner; J. Djumalieva; D. Copple; and J. Thurgood. 2019. Transforming Naturally Occurring Text Data into Economic Statistics: The Case of Online Job Vacancy Postings. *NBER Working Paper Series No. 25837*. National Bureau of Economic Research. https://doi.org/10.3386/w25837.

UN Women. 2020. *World Survey on the Role of Women in Development 2019: Why Addressing Women's Income and Time Poverty Matters for Sustainable Development.* https://www.unwomen.org/sites/default/files/Headquarters/Attachments/Sections/Library/Publications/2019/World-survey-on-the-role-of-women-in-development-2019.pdf.

West, M.; R. Kraut; and H. E. Chew. 2019. *I'd Blush If I Could: Closing Gender Divides in Digital Skills through Education.* UNESCO and EQUALS Skills Coalition. https://en.unesco.org/Id-blush-if-I-could.

World Bank. 2019a. Malaysia's 'Critical Occupations List' is an Innovative Tool for Preparing Workers for the Jobs of the Future. Press release. September 12. https://www.worldbank.org/en/news/press-release/2019/09/12/malaysias-critical-occupations-list-is-an-innovative-tool-for-preparing-workers-for-the-jobs-of-the-future-world-bank.

———. 2019b. *Systematic Country Diagnostic of the Philippines: Realizing the Filipino Dream for 2040.* Washington, DC. https://openknowledge.worldbank.org/handle/10986/32646.

———. 2020. *Indonesia's Critical Occupations List 2018.* https://documents1.worldbank.org/curated/en/763611585857010121/pdf/Indonesias-Critical-Occupations-List-2018-Technical-Report.pdf.

Xu, T.; H. Zhu; C. Zhu; P. Li; and H. Xiong. 2017. Measuring the Popularity of Job Skills in Recruitment Market: A Multi-criteria Approach. *Proceedings of the AAAI Conference on Artificial Intelligence.* 32(1). https://doi.org/10.1609/aaai.v32i1.11847.

Yamauchi, F.; S. Nomura; S. Imaizumi; A. C. Areias; and A. R. Chowdhury. 2018. Asymmetric Information on Noncognitive Skills in the Indian Labor Market: An Experiment in Online Job Portal. *Policy Research Working Paper No. 8378*. World Bank. http://hdl.handle.net/10986/29558.